STARS

EARLY BIRD
ASTRONOMY

BY GREGORY L. VOGT

LERNER PUBLICATIONS COMPANY • MINNEAPOLIS

Lerner Publications Company
A division of Lerner Publishing Group, Inc.
241 First Avenue North
Minneapolis, MN 55401 U.S.A.

Website address: www.lernerbooks.com

Library of Congress Cataloging-in-Publication Data

Vogt, Gregory.
    Stars / by Gregory L. Vogt.
       p.   cm. — (Early bird astronomy)
    Includes index.
    ISBN 978–0–7613–3873–4 (lib. bdg. : alk. paper)
    1. Stars—Juvenile literature. I. Title.
QB801.7.V634 2010
523.8—dc22   2009016896

Manufactured in the United States of America
1 – BP – 12/15/09

CONTENTS

BE A WORD DETECTIVE

Can you find these words as you read about stars? Be a detective and try to figure out what they mean. You can turn to the glossary on page 46 for help.

astronomers	constellations	orbit
atmosphere	galaxy	rotate
axis	gravity	satellite
black hole	light-year	solar system
cluster	nebulas	telescope

Thousands of stars twinkle in the night sky. What are stars made of?

CHAPTER 1

STARS NIGHT AND DAY

Look toward the sky on a clear night. Stars are everywhere! Some appear bright. Other stars seem dim. They are many different colors.

A star is a huge ball of gases. The gases press on the star's center. This produces great amounts of heat and light. The heat and light leave the star's surface and travel through space.

The light from a star makes its way to Earth. We can see the light in the sky.

You can see light from stars during the night and the day. At night, you can see thousands of stars. Most stars appear as tiny points of light. That is because they are very far away from Earth. The other stars are too dim to see without a telescope (TEH-luh-skohp). A telescope is a tool that makes far-off objects seem brighter and closer.

Telescopes give us a better look at objects in space.

The Sun is a star. It gives us light and heat.

During the day, you can see just one star. It is our Sun. The Sun is the closest star to Earth. So we see it as a giant glowing ball. It is so bright that staring at it is bad for our eyes!

During the day, sunlight lights up the sky. You cannot see light from stars that are farther away.

We cannot see other stars during the day because of light from the Sun. Sunlight makes Earth's atmosphere (AT-muhs-feer) glow. The atmosphere is made of the gases that surround Earth.

Watch the sky every night. What do you notice? You may see the stars moving across the sky from east to west. During the day, the Sun also crosses the sky.

Stars appear in different places in the sky throughout the night. These two photos were taken 45 minutes apart. Lines have been added in these pictures to show two of the star patterns in the sky.

Long ago, people thought the sky was moving. In modern times, we know that the stars and the Sun appear to move because Earth rotates. To rotate means to spin. Earth rotates around an imaginary line called an axis (AK-sihs). As Earth rotates, the stars appear to move slowly across the sky.

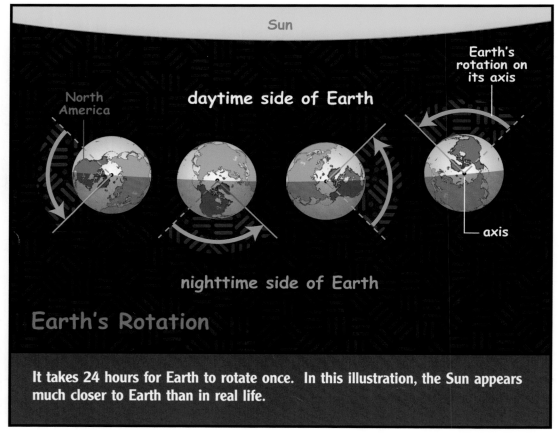

Sun

Earth's rotation on its axis

North America

daytime side of Earth

axis

nighttime side of Earth

Earth's Rotation

It takes 24 hours for Earth to rotate once. In this illustration, the Sun appears much closer to Earth than in real life.

This is a photo of star trails. They show how stars appear to move across the night sky when Earth rotates.

To understand how stars appear to move, try this. Pretend you are Earth. Slowly turn to the left. The room appears to move to the right. Then slowly turn to the right. The room appears to move to the left.

The Sun disappears in the evening as Earth rotates away from it. How far is the Sun from Earth?

CHAPTER 2
OUR STAR

Scientists who study objects in space are called astronomers (uh-STRAH-nuh-muhrs). They use special telescopes and other tools to study the stars and space. Astronomers have learned a lot about stars by studying the Sun.

The Sun looks different from nighttime stars because it is much closer to Earth. Astronomers have figured out that the Sun is about 93 million miles (150 million kilometers) away. If you could ride a jet plane from Earth to the Sun, it would take about 21 years to get there.

This photo shows how the Sun and Earth look from space.

Compared to other stars, the Sun is close. The next nearest star is actually a group of three stars. The brightest star in this group is Alpha Centauri. It is about 24 trillion (24,000,000,000,000) miles (39 trillion km) away. It would take about 5.5 million years on the same jet plane to get there! All other stars are much farther from Earth.

From Earth, Alpha Centauri looks like just one star. This photo taken from space shows two of the three stars that make up this group.

Sirius A is the brightest star in the nighttime sky. It is 8.6 light-years away from Earth.

Astronomers measure distances in light-years. A light-year is the distance light travels in one year. One light-year is about 6 trillion miles (10 trillion km). Saying that Alpha Centauri is about 4 light-years away is easier than saying that it is 24 trillion miles (39 trillion km) away.

The Sun is a medium-sized star. It is 864,000 miles (1.4 million km) across. That is 110 times wider than Earth. But the Sun is small compared to some stars. The star Betelgeuse is 1,200 times bigger than the Sun. Other stars are only about the size of Earth.

This artwork shows the Sun's size as compared to Earth and other planets. Earth is the third planet from the Sun.

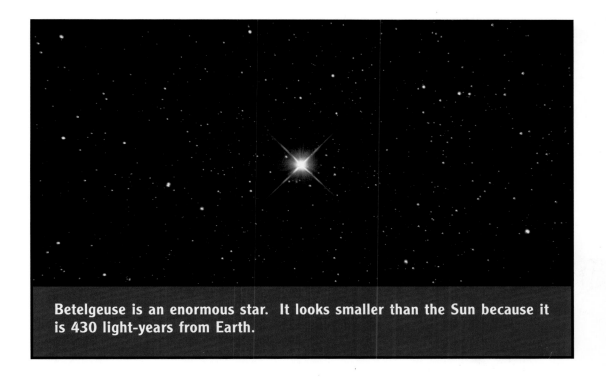

Betelgeuse is an enormous star. It looks smaller than the Sun because it is 430 light-years from Earth.

The Sun and other stars are made mostly of gases. Imagine the Sun as a giant pie cut into 10 slices. Nine slices would be made of hydrogen gas. One slice would be helium gas. The leftover crumbs would be materials such as iron, nickel, and oxygen.

The Sun's gravity holds together all the materials that make up the Sun. Gravity is a force that attracts all things to one another.

The heat from the Sun warms Earth.

Deep inside the Sun, the weight of the gases pressing down on the center does amazing things. It can change about 4 million tons (3.6 million metric tons) of hydrogen into helium every second. This process produces light and heat. The light and heat we experience every day were created inside the Sun.

The Sun's surface looks like it is on fire. But it is not burning. Very hot glowing gases on the surface boil and splash. Tongues of gas shoot out and fall back.

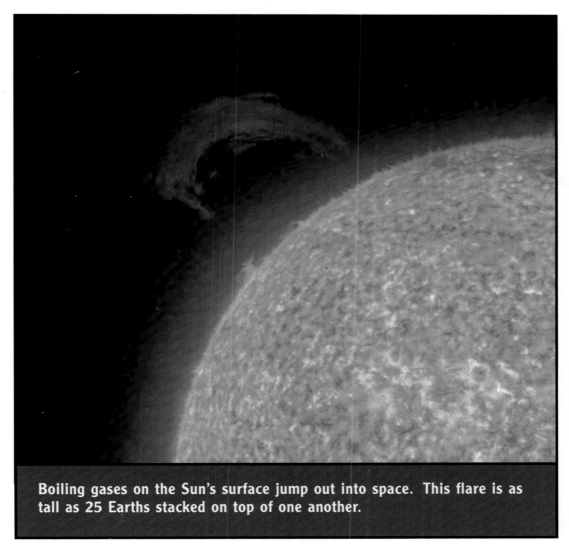

Boiling gases on the Sun's surface jump out into space. This flare is as tall as 25 Earths stacked on top of one another.

The color of a star has to do with how hot its surface is. Stars can be blue, white, yellow, orange, and red. Our Sun is a whitish yellow star. It is about 10,000°F (5,500°C) at its surface. That's about 25 times hotter than the temperature

Stars can be many colors. What colors do you see in this photo?

you'd use to cook a pizza. Astronomers know that other whitish yellow stars are about the same temperature as the Sun. Some blue stars can be as hot as 100,000°F (55,500°C) at their surface. Red stars are only about 4,000°F (2,200°C).

Regulus is a bright blue star. Parts of it can get as hot as 27,000°F (15,000°C).

From Earth, the Milky Way looks like a cloudy band of stars. How many stars are in the Milky Way?

CHAPTER 3

NEIGHBORHOOD OF STARS

Our Sun has many neighbors in space. Most of them are stars. Dust, gases, planets, and moons are also nearby. All of these objects are part of the Sun's galaxy.

The Sun's galaxy is called the Milky Way. In the night sky, its edge looks like a milky path. From space, it looks like a bright pinwheel. There are between 200 and 400 billion stars in the Milky Way!

All the stars in the Milky Way orbit around its center. To orbit means to circle around. The gravity of all the stars keeps the Milky Way together as the galaxy moves in space.

The Milky Way looks like a pinwheel from space.

As stars orbit the galaxy's center, small groups of stars also circle around one another. Two stars orbit the North Star. You need a telescope to see this.

Polaris B

Polaris Ab

Polaris A

The North Star is also called Polaris. It is part of a three-star system.

The seven brightest stars in this photo make up part of the star cluster Pleiades.

There are big clusters of stars in the Milky Way too. They are held together by gravity. One cluster that is easy to see is called the Pleiades. It contains about 1,000 stars. Other clusters have more than 100,000 stars. Some even have millions of stars.

Sometimes, planets orbit a single star. Eight planets orbit our Sun. Moons and other space objects orbit the planets. Together, the planets, the moons, and the objects that orbit the Sun make up our solar system.

Planets are smaller than most stars. So it can be hard to see planets orbiting stars. But astronomers have discovered hundreds of planets around other stars. It is possible that most stars have planets orbiting them.

This illustration shows the planets orbiting the Sun.

This photo was taken by a powerful space telescope. It shows thousands of new stars being born. How long do stars live?

CHAPTER 4
THE BEGINNING AND THE END

Stars aren't alive, but astronomers talk about them as if they were. Astronomers speak of stars' life cycles. Stars are born. They live for millions or billions of years. Then they die.

This dark cloud of gas and dust is known as the Horsehead Nebula. The bright areas are light from new stars.

There are huge clouds of gas and dust throughout the Milky Way. These clouds are called nebulas (NEH-byuh-luhs). Stars are born in the biggest nebulas. Stars can take millions of years to form.

Gravity causes the gases in nebulas to collect into many clumps. As the clumps get bigger in size, their gravity becomes stronger. More gases fall into the clumps. Then they start to spin. Beginning stars become very hot. The clumps keep collecting gases. When they are large enough, gases in their centers begin changing. They release heat and light. That is how stars are born.

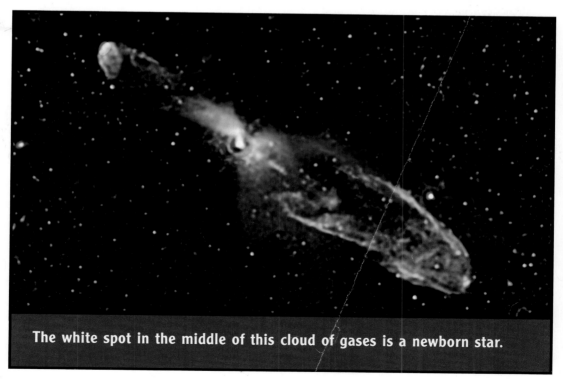

The white spot in the middle of this cloud of gases is a newborn star.

The size of the new star and how much material it contains determines how bright it will be. Really big, massive stars can be one thousand times brighter and much hotter than our Sun. We wouldn't want Earth to orbit a star like that. We'd be cooked!

An artist made this illustration of a giant blue star.

Ancient astronomers observed this star exploding in 1572. More than four hundred years later, hot gases and other materials still are visible.

The size and the amount of material a star contains also affect how long a star will live. Really big and bright stars last only about 100 million years. They use up their hydrogen gas much faster than stars like our Sun do. At the end of their lives, they expand and explode. They leave behind a new cloud of gas and other materials. In millions or billions of years, the cloud will form new stars.

This dying star releases colorful gases. It will leave behind a dim white star at its center.

How long will a star like the Sun last? The Sun was born about five billion years ago. Astronomers expect it to live another five billion years. When the Sun runs out of hydrogen, it will expand. It will get so large that its gases will destroy all the planets as far out as Jupiter. All that will be left of the Sun will be a heavy ball of material in the center. This ball will become a dim white star about the size of a large planet.

Stars that are larger than the Sun may have a different end. They may collapse into a very tiny space. Their gravity becomes so great that anything that comes near them is dragged inward. Even light near the dying star is dragged in. Stars that have this end are called black holes.

The gravity of black holes can drag many nearby stars into it. Astronomers think a supersized black hole is at the center of the Milky Way.

An artist created this illustration of a black hole.

CHAPTER 5

STUDYING THE STARS

When people first studied the stars, the skies were much clearer. There were few city lights and little pollution. So the sky at night appeared very dark. People could see thousands of stars sparkling like jewels in the sky.

From the beginning, people imagined that stars formed groups. They noticed that if they connected the stars in the group, they could see patterns. These patterns are called constellations (cahn-stuh-LAY-shunz). People named the constellations after gods, animals, and other familiar things.

This illustration shows the star patterns that early stargazers saw in the night sky.

In modern times, lights from cities make it harder to see many stars at night. If you want to see the sky the way ancient people did, go to the country. Find a place far away from lights. Bring a star map and a flashlight.

Can you find any stars in this photo of the night sky?

A star map helps you find constellations. Lines on star maps show which stars belong to a constellation. If you are looking for a particular star, find its constellation. Betelgeuse is a reddish giant star. It is found in the left shoulder of Orion the Hunter. Orion is an easy constellation to find. When you find Orion, you find Betelgeuse.

This photograph shows lines connecting the stars in the constellation Orion. Betelgeuse is labeled on the upper left.

Astronomers use more than their eyes and star maps to study stars. They use powerful telescopes and other special instruments. These tools allow them to see stars that are too dim to see with just their eyes.

Astronomers use high-powered equipment to get a better look at faraway stars.

These telescopes sit at the top of a mountain in Chile.

The telescopes astronomers use are huge. Some are wider than a classroom. Many are built on top of mountains. These telescopes are away from city lights. The air is also thinner and cleaner on top of mountains. So it is easier to see light from stars.

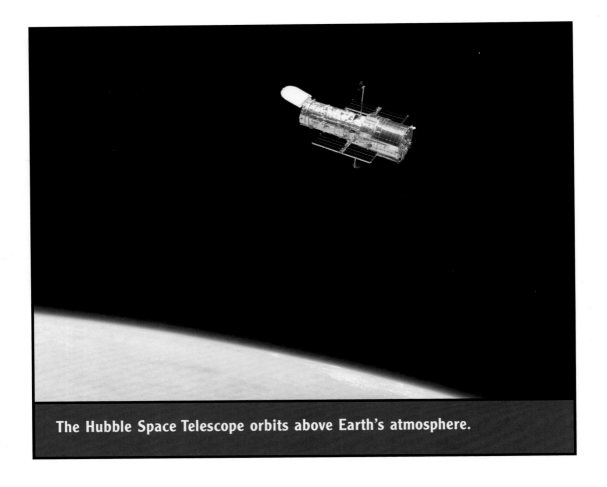

The Hubble Space Telescope orbits above Earth's atmosphere.

One of the most exciting tools astronomers use to study the stars is the Hubble Space Telescope (HST). The HST is a satellite (SA-tuh-lite) that orbits Earth above its atmosphere. The HST has a much clearer view of objects in space than telescopes on Earth do.

Using the HST, astronomers have studied thousands of stars, galaxies, and nebulas. They have seen the beginnings and the ends of stars. They have looked billions of light-years into space and discovered thousands of galaxies like our own.

The HST took this photo of a star cluster that lies two thousand light-years beyond the Sun.

LEARN MORE ABOUT
STARS

BOOKS

Driscoll, Michael. *A Child's Introduction to the Night Sky: The Story of the Stars, Planets, and Constellations—and How You Can Find Them.* New York: Black Dog & Leventhal Publishers, 2004. Find out more about the Sun, planets, stars, and galaxies as well as tips for stargazing.

Graun, Ken. *Our Constellations and Their Stars.* Tucson, AZ: Ken Press, 2004. Read answers to questions about stars, stargazing, and constellations.

Rey, Hans Augusto. *Find the Constellation.* 2nd ed. Boston: Houghton Mifflin Harcourt, 2008. Learn about the constellations and where to look for different stars.

Stott, Carole. *Astronomy: Discoveries, Solar System, Stars, Universe.* Boston: Kingfisher, 2003. Discover more about the solar system, stars, galaxies, and the search for life in space.

WEBSITES

HubbleSite
http://hubblesite.org/
Here you can see photographs taken by NASA's Hubble Space Telescope and much more.

Stars and Galaxies
http://www.jpl.nasa.gov/stars-galaxies/index.cfm
This is a site operated by NASA's Jet Propulsion Laboratory. You will find information on astronomy missions and their discoveries.

Your Sky
http://www.fourmilab.ch/yoursky/
This site gives you a current star map for your night sky. The map has many controls, and you can change what you see.

GLOSSARY

astronomers (uh-STRAH-nuh-muhrz): scientists who study planets, stars, and other things in space

atmosphere (AT-muhs-feer): the layer of gases that surrounds Earth

axis (AK-sihs): an imaginary line that goes through a planet from top to bottom. Earth spins around its axis.

black hole: a mass of material so great and so compact that its gravity pulls in nearby objects and even light

cluster: a close group of hundreds, thousands, or even millions of stars

constellations (cahn-stuh-LAY-shunz): groups of stars in the sky that represent people, things, or animals

galaxy: a group of billions of stars that swirl around one another and are held together by their combined gravity

gravity: a force that causes all objects to be attracted to one another

light-year: the distance light travels in one year. That's about 6 trillion miles (10 trillion km).

nebulas (NEH-byuh-luhz): giant clouds of gas and dust in space that glow from the light of stars inside them

orbit: to travel in a circle around another object in space. Orbit can also mean the path of a star, a planet, a moon, or other object as it travels around a sun or a planet.

rotate: to spin around an axis

satellite (SA-tuh-lite): an object that circles around a larger object in space

solar system: the collection of planets, moons, and other objects that orbit the Sun

telescope (TEH-luh-skohp): an instrument that makes farawy objects appear bigger and closer

INDEX

Pages listed in **bold** type refer to photographs.

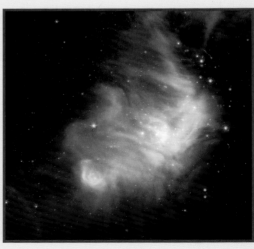